STEP·BY·STEP

ITALIAN
Cooking

KÖNEMANN

SOUPS & STARTERS

Italian family meals generally start with a simple antipasto. This can be a
selection of salami, seafoods, olives, cheeses and piquant bottled vegetables.

Seafood Tomato Soup

Preparation time:
   20 minutes
Cooking time:
   15 minutes
Serves 4

1½ pounds mussels in shell	*2 cloves garlic, crushed*
1½ pounds prawns or large shrimp	*2 small red chilies, finely chopped*
1 pound boneless fish fillets	*8 cups fish or chicken broth*
8 ounces small squid or calamari tubes	*14½-ounce can whole tomatoes, undrained, crushed*
¼ cup olive oil	*⅓ cup chopped parsley*
1 onion, chopped	*¼ cup tomato paste*
1 cup sliced fresh fennel	

---

1 Scrub and debeard mussels. Add to a pan of simmering water. Cover and simmer 5 minutes or till shells open, discarding any that do not open. Remove mussels from shells. Reserve four shells for garnish.

2 Peel and devein prawns and cut fish into bite-size pieces. Slice squid into rings; set aside.

3 In a large saucepan heat olive oil. Cook onion, fennel, garlic, and chilies in hot oil till onion is tender.

4 Add broth, tomatoes, parsley and tomato paste. Bring to a boil; reduce heat. Cover; simmer for 5 minutes.

5 Add mussels, prawns, fish and squid. Simmer, uncovered, 3 to 5 minutes or till prawns turn pink and fish flakes. Garnish with reserved shells.

Use scissors to remove cooked mussels from shells.

Cube fish, peel and devein prawns and slice squid or calamari into rings.

Add finely chopped parsley to soup.
Simmer for 5 minutes.

Add prepared seafood and simmer
gently 3 to 5 minutes.

3

Meatball, Bean and Macaroni Soup

Preparation time:
  20 minutes
Cooking time:
  30 minutes
Serves 6

---

1 pound lean ground
  beef
1¼ cups soft bread
  crumbs
½ cup tomato paste
2 teaspoons dried
  oregano, crushed
8 cups chicken broth

2 onions, chopped
2 potatoes, chopped
2 carrots, chopped
⅔ cup macaroni
15-ounce can kidney
  beans, drained
1¼ cups fresh shelled
  peas or frozen peas

---

1 In a bowl combine ground beef, bread crumbs, tomato paste and oregano. Shape mixture into bite-size meatballs.

2 In a large skillet cook meatballs in hot oil 8 minutes or till no pink remains, turning to brown evenly. Drain well.

3 In a saucepan combine broth, onions, potatoes and carrots. Bring to a boil; reduce heat. Add macaroni. Cover; simmer 10 minutes or till macaroni is al dente.

4 Add meatballs, kidney beans and peas. Simmer 5 minutes.

Knead ground beef, bread crumbs, tomato paste and oregano till smooth.

Drain cooked meatballs on paper towels.

Add macaroni to soup mixture and cook until tender.

Stir in meatballs, kidney beans and peas. Simmer for 5 minutes.

Golden Fried Sole with Sambuca

Preparation time:
10 minutes
Cooking time:
6 minutes
Serves 4

---

1 pound skinless sole or orange roughy fillets, ½-inch thick
all-purpose flour
2 eggs
¼ cup finely chopped parsley
freshly ground pepper

¼ cup grated parmesan cheese
¼ cup sambuca or Pernod
¼ cup butter
lemon wedges
parsley sprigs

---

1 Rinse fish and pat dry with paper towels. Dust lightly with flour. Set aside.

2 In a bowl combine eggs, chopped parsley, pepper, parmesan and sambuca. Add fish to egg mixture, tossing to coat.

3 In a large skillet melt butter over medium heat. Add fish to hot butter in a single layer. Cook fish about 3 minutes on each side or till golden brown and fish flakes easily.

4 Drain fish on paper towels. Serve with lemon wedges and parsley sprigs.

Rinse fish fillets and dust lightly with flour.

Coat flour-dusted fish with egg mixture.

Pan-fry sole in a single layer until golden brown.

Fish is done when it flakes easily when tested with a fork.

Mixed Antipasto Platter

Preparation time:
45 minutes
Cooking time:
30 minutes
Serves 4

Frittata Wedges
4 eggs
³/₄ cup light cream
¹/₄ cup grated
  Parmesan cheese
6 slices Italian
  salami, chopped
1 tablespoon chopped
  fresh basil

Broiled Mussels
1 pound mussels in
  shell

¹/₄ cup lemon juice
1 clove garlic, crushed
1 small red chili,
  finely chopped
chopped parsley

calamata olives
marinated artichoke
  hearts
sliced tomatoes
fresh mozzarella
  cheese
fresh basil

---

1 For frittata, in a bowl combine eggs and cream till well combined. Stir in Parmesan cheese, salami and basil.

2 Spoon mixture into a greased 8-inch pie plate and bake in a 350° oven for 25 minutes or till set. Cool; cut into small wedges to serve.

3 For mussels, scrub and debeard mussels. Place in saucepan of simmering water. Cover and simmer for 5 minutes or till shells open, discarding any that do not open.

4 Open mussels completely and loosen from shells using scissors. Return mussels to half shells.

5 Combine lemon juice, garlic and chili; spoon over mussels. Broil 4 inches from heat 1 to 2 minutes or till heated through. Sprinkle with parsley.

6 To serve: On a large serving platter arrange frittata wedges, mussels, olives, artichoke hearts, tomatoes, and mozzarella slices. Garnish with basil.

For frittatas, combine eggs and cream. Stir in Parmesan, salami, and basil.

Spoon mixture into a greased 8-inch pie plate.

For mussels, spoon lemon juice, garlic and chili mixture over mussels.

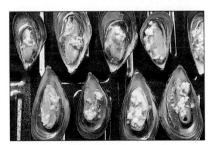

Place mussels on unheated broiler rack. Broil until heated through.

Herb-Marinated Red Bell Peppers

4 red bell peppers
²/₃ cup olive oil
¹/₄ cup lemon juice
1 tablespoon chopped fresh basil
1 tablespoon parsley
2 teaspoons chopped fresh oregano
8 arugula leaves
8 Romaine lettuce leaves
8 ounces feta cheese

Preparation time:
    20 minutes +
    2 hours marinating
Cooking time:
    3 minutes
Serves 4

1 Cut peppers into quarters; remove stems, seeds and membranes. Broil peppers, skin side up, about 3 inches from heat till skin blisters and turns black.

2 Using tongs, place peppers in a brown paper bag; seal and let stand for 15 to 20 minutes. Gently pull skin off. Cut peppers into strips.

3 Place strips in a bowl. Combine olive oil, lemon juice, basil, parsley, and oregano. Pour over peppers. Cover; marinate 2 hours at room temperature or refrigerate overnight.

4 To serve, arrange peppers, arugula, Romaine and cubes of feta cheese on serving plates.

Cut red bell peppers into quarters; remove stems, seeds and membranes.

Carefully peel away blistered skin from roasted peppers.

Cut the peppers into ¾-inch wide strips.

Pour the olive oil mixture over red pepper strips. Cover and marinate.

Carpaccio

12 ounces beef
  tenderloin
olive oil
1 small piece fresh
  Parmesan cheese
  (about 4 ounces)
freshly ground pepper
salt (optional)
lemon wedges

1 Wrap beef in plastic wrap; place in freezer about 2 hours or till firm but not

Preparation time:
  20 minutes
Cooking time:
  None
Serves 4

frozen solid. Using a sharp knife, trim fat from beef. Slice partially frozen beef into wafer thin slices. Arrange beef on serving plates.
2 Drizzle oil lightly over beef slices. Using a vegetable peeler, shave thin pieces of cheese from

Parmesan. Sprinkle cheese over beef.
3 Season beef with pepper and, if desired, salt. Serve with lemon wedges.

Note: Choose the best quality beef available for this recipe. Toppings may be served separately.

HINT
Ask your butcher or local delicatessen to slice the beef into wafer-thin slices with their slicing machine.

Trim beef of any fat. With sharp knife, cut meat into wafer-thin slices.

Arrange beef slices in a single layer on a serving plate.

Drizzle good-quality olive oil evenly over beef slices.

Use a vegetable peeler to shave thin slices of Parmesan over beef.

VEGETABLES & SALADS

Vegetables play a major role in Italian meals. They are served as antipasto, with pasta and as side dishes. Most popular are eggplant, red bell peppers, and zucchini.

Genoese Bean and Potato Bake

1 pound baking potatoes
1 pound fresh green beans
2 eggs, lightly beaten
2/3 cup grated Parmesan cheese
1/4 cup chopped Italian parsley
1/4 cup chopped dill
freshly ground pepper
1 1/4 cups soft bread crumbs
1/4 cup olive oil

Preparation time:
  20 minutes
Cooking time:
  30 minutes
Serves 6

1 Peel and coarsely chop potatoes. Cook potatoes in saucepan of boiling water about 20 minutes or till tender. Drain and mash. Set aside.

2 Meanwhile, trim and coarsely chop beans. Cook beans in saucepan of boiling water 20 minutes or till tender. Drain. Place in a food processor and blend till coarsely mashed.

3 In a bowl combine potatoes, beans, eggs, Parmesan, parsley, dill and pepper.

4 Spoon mixture into six ramekins or one 8-inch pie plate. Toss together bread crumbs and oil; sprinkle over mixture. Bake, uncovered, in 350° oven 30 minutes or till heated through and lightly browned. Serve with grilled or roasted meats.

HINT
Use a potato masher to mash potatoes because a food processor or blender will make them sticky and gluey.

Mash cooked potatoes without milk or butter until smooth.

Process cooked green beans until coarsely mashed.

Combine potatoes, beans, eggs, Parmesan, parsley, dill and pepper.

To make soft breadcrumbs, process crustless bread in processor.

...alad ...nd ...ts

Preparation time:
15 minutes
Cooking time:
10 minutes
Serves 4

---

2 slices white or whole grain bread
2 tablespoons butter or margarine
2 slices bacon, chopped
1/2 head Romaine lettuce
2 ounces gorgonzola or blue cheese, crumbled

1/2 cup coarsely chopped walnuts
1 egg
1/2 cup olive oil
1 tablespoon lemon juice
2 canned anchovy fillets, drained
1 teaspoon prepared mustard

---

1 To make croutons, remove crusts from bread and cut into 1/2-inch cubes. In a skillet melt butter or margarine and cook bread cubes in hot butter till crisp and brown. Drain on paper towels.

2 In same skillet cook bacon till brown and crisp. Drain on paper towels.

3 Wash and dry lettuce and tear into bite-size pieces. In a large bowl combine lettuce, croutons, bacon, cheese, and walnuts; toss well.

4 For dressing, gently lower egg into simmering water and cook for 1 minute. Remove from water and crack egg into a food processor or blender container. Add oil, lemon juice, anchovies, and mustard. Cover and process or blend till smooth. Pour over salad and toss; serve immediately.

HINT
The best type of oil to use in salads dressings is extra virgin olive oil which is made from the first pressing of the olives. This slightly green oil is thicker and has a richer flavor and aroma than other olive oils. Use other olive oils for cooking.

For croutons, cook bread cubes in butter or margarine until golden brown.

Cook bacon in skillet till crisp and brown.

Wash and dry lettuce and break it into bite-size pieces.

Combine lettuce with croutons, bacon, cheese, and walnuts.

17

Cauliflower Neapolitan

½ head cauliflower
14½-ounce can whole tomatoes
1 tablespoon olive oil
1 onion, finely chopped
12 pimiento-stuffed green olives, sliced
2 teaspoons chopped capers
½ teaspoon sugar

Preparation time:
15 minutes
Cooking time:
10 minutes
Serves 4

1 Cut cauliflower into large flowerets. Cook in boiling water about 10 minutes or till tender. Drain in a colander and rinse with cold water.

2 Place undrained tomatoes in food processor or blender container. Cover and process till smooth.

Strain out seeds.

3 In a large skillet heat olive oil. Cook onion in hot oil till tender. Add puréed tomatoes, olives, capers, and sugar. Cook over low heat till heated through.

4 Add cauliflower and toss till well coated. Serve immediately.

Serve with roasted or grilled meat or as a part of an antipasto platter.

Wash cauliflower and cut into large flowerets.

Strain processed tomatoes through a fine sieve to remove the seeds.

Add sliced olives and capers to tomato sauce.

Add cooked cauliflower to sauce and serve immediately.

Ratatouille with Baked Polenta

Preparation time:
    30 minutes
Cooking time:
    30 minutes
Serves 4

Baked Polenta
1 cup self-rising flour
1 cup coarse or stone
    ground cornmeal
1/3 cup shredded
    cheddar cheese
3/4 cup milk
1/4 cup butter, melted
1 egg, lightly beaten

Ratatouille
1 large eggplant
4 medium zucchini

1/4 cup olive oil
1 onion, sliced
2 cloves garlic,
    crushed
3 large ripe tomatoes,
    peeled and chopped
1 green bell pepper,
    sliced
3/4 cup water
1/3 cup tomato paste
2 teaspoons sugar
1 teaspoon dried
    oregano, crushed

---

1 For polenta, in a bowl combine flour, cornmeal, and cheese. Make a well in center.
2 Stir together milk, butter or margarine, and egg; add to flour mixture and stir till well combined.
3 Pour mixture into a greased 8-inch pie plate. Bake, uncovered, in a 350° oven for 25 minutes or till light brown.
4 For ratatouille, slice eggplant about 1/2-inch thick. Cut slices into strips about 2 inches long. Cut zucchini lengthwise into 1/2-inch thick slices; cut slices into strips about 2 inches long.
5 In a large saucepan or skillet heat oil. Cook onion and garlic in hot oil till onion is tender.
6 Add eggplant, zucchini, tomatoes, bell pepper, water, tomato paste, sugar, and oregano. Bring to a boil; reduce heat. Cover and simmer for 15 minutes or till vegetables are tender. Serve with wedges of polenta.

Add milk, butter, and egg mixture to flour mixture and stir till well combined.

Spoon the batter into a greased 8-inch pie plate.

Cut eggplant and zucchini into long strips about ½-inch thick.

Combine all vegetables in pan; add water, paste, sugar and oregano.

PASTA, RICE & PIZZA

To many people, Italian cooking means pasta. It can be served simply with a little butter and cheese or with a rich sauce.

Spaghetti Puttanesca

Preparation time:
15 minutes
Cooking time:
15 minutes
Serves 4

---

4 large ripe tomatoes (about 1¹/₂ pounds)
1 tablespoon olive oil
2 small red chilies, chopped
2 cloves garlic, crushed
²/₃ cup water
12 pitted ripe olives, sliced
8 canned anchovy fillets, drained and chopped
¹/₄ cup chopped parsley
1 tablespoon chopped fresh basil or 1 teaspoon dried
2 teaspoons chopped capers
8 ounces dried spaghetti
freshly grated parmesan (optional)
Italian parsley (optional)

---

1 Peel, seed and chop tomatoes.
2 In a saucepan heat oil over medium heat. Cook chilies and garlic in hot oil for 1 minute. Add tomatoes and water. Bring to a boil; reduce heat. Cover; simmer 10 minutes or till tomatoes are soft. Add additional water if sauce sticks to pan during cooking.
3 Add olives, anchovies, parsley, basil and capers to saucepan. Simmer, uncovered, for 3 minutes.
4 Meanwhile, cook spaghetti till al dente. Drain. Add to tomato mixture; toss till combined. If desired, sprinkle each serving with grated parmesan; garnish with parsley.

Peel tomatoes and remove seeds with a teaspoon.

Add water to tomato mixture. Cover and simmer for 10 minutes.

Add olives, anchovies, parsley, basil, and capers to tomato mixture.

Toss cooked spaghetti and sauce mixture till well combined.

Spinach, Mushroom and Ham Lasagna

Preparation time:
  15 minutes
Cooking time:
  15 minutes
Serves 4

16 large spinach leaves	*14½-ounce can diced tomatoes*
8 ounces ricotta cheese	*1½ cups tomato purée*
⅔ cup shredded cheddar cheese	*¼ cup chopped fresh basil*
¼ cup olive oil	*9 lasagna noodles*
1 onion, chopped	*½ cup grated parmesan cheese*
2 cloves garlic, crushed	*1 cup shredded mozzarella cheese*
8 ounces mushrooms	
6 ounces ham, chopped	

1 Coarsely chop spinach. Place in steamer basket over boiling water. Cover; steam 3 to 5 minutes or till tender; drain. In a bowl combine spinach, ricotta and cheddar; set aside.

2 In a large skillet heat oil. Cook onion and garlic in hot oil till onion is tender. Add chopped mushrooms and ham; cook till mushrooms are tender. Stir in tomatoes and purée.

Bring to a boil; reduce heat. Simmer, uncovered, for 10 to 20 minutes. Stir in basil.

3 Meanwhile, cook lasagna till al dente; drain.

4 Layer half the cooked lasagna noodles in 12 x 7½ x 2-inch baking pan. Spread with half of the spinach mixture. Top with half of the ham mixture. Repeat layers. Sprinkle parmesan on top.

5 Cover and bake in a 350° oven for 25 minutes. Uncover and bake 10 minutes more or till heated through. Sprinkle with mozzarella cheese. Let stand 10 minutes.

Combine spinach, ricotta cheese, and cheddar cheese. Mix well.

Add diced tomatoes and tomato purée to ham and mushroom mixture.

Spread half of the spinach mixture over the lasagna noodles.

Top spinach mixture with half of the ham mixture and repeat layers.

Penne Pasta with Creamy Seafood Sauce

*1 pound prawns or
large shrimp*
*12 ounces white fish
fillets*
8 ounces bay scallops
*3 ounces smoked
salmon*
2 cups chicken broth
6 tablespoons butter
1 onion, chopped
1 clove garlic, crushed
*3 tablespoons
all-purpose flour*
4 egg yolks
2/3 cup heavy cream
2 teaspoons lemon juice
1 pound penne pasta
*1 tablespoon chopped
fresh basil or
1 teaspoon dried
fresh basil leaves*

Preparation time:
20 minutes
Cooking time:
40 minutes
Serves 6

1 Peel and devein prawns. Cut fish into 1-inch cubes. Rinse scallops; pat dry with paper towels. Cut salmon into strips.
2 In a saucepan bring chicken broth to a boil. Add shrimp; cook 1 to 2 minutes or till shrimp turn pink. Remove. Add fish; simmer for 1 to 2 minutes or till tender when tested with a fork. Remove. Add scallops; simmer 1 to 2 minutes or till tender. Remove. Set broth and cooked fish and seafood aside.

3 In a saucepan melt butter. Add onion and garlic; cook till onion is tender. Stir in flour.
4 Add reserved chicken broth. Cook till thickened. Cook and stir 10 minutes or till reduced by one-third. In a small bowl beat yolks, cream, and lemon juice.
5 Remove sauce from heat. Slowly stir in egg mixture, beating constantly. Return to heat; stir over low heat till heated through (do not boil). Cook pasta till al dente. Drain.
6 Place fish, seafood and salmon in bowl. Pour sauce over, stir in basil. Pour over hot pasta to serve.

Peel and devein prawns, cut fish into cubes, rinse scallops, and slice salmon.

Add chicken broth all at once to onion mixture.

Slowly stir egg yolk mixture into sauce, beating to prevent curdling.

Toss together seafood mixture and sauce till well coated.

Ravioli with Browned Butter and Pecorino

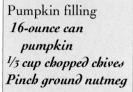

Pumpkin filling
16-ounce can pumpkin
1/3 cup chopped chives
Pinch ground nutmeg

Ravioli dough
3 cups all-purpose flour
pinch salt
4 eggs, lightly beaten
1 egg, lightly beaten

Sauce
1/2 cup butter or margarine
freshly grated pecorino or parmesan cheese
chives

Preparation time:
1 hour
Cooking time:
5 minutes
Serves 4

1 For filling, in a bowl combine pumpkin, chopped chives, and nutmeg. Set aside.

2 For ravioli dough, in a bowl stir together flour and salt. Make a well in the center. Add the four beaten eggs. With a fork, gradually stir together the flour and eggs. Turn dough out onto a lightly floured surface and knead about 5 minutes or till dough is smooth and elastic. Cover and let rest for 5 minutes.

3 Divide dough into four portions. Roll out one portion of dough with a rolling pin or pasta machine till dough is a thin rectangle. Roll out another section of dough to a thin rectangle slightly larger than the first.

4 On the smaller rectangle, place teaspoonsful of filling at 2-inch intervals in rows across the dough. Brush the dough between the filling very lightly with the remaining beaten egg. Place second sheet of dough carefully over top. Press dough between the filling to seal the dough together.

5 Use a floured crimped pastry wheel or sharp knife to cut dough into squares between the mounds of filling. Place squares of ravioli in a single layer on a lightly floured tray; cover until ready to cook.

6 Cook ravioli in a large pot of boiling water. Cook about 4 minutes or till tender. Drain. Transfer to a serving plate and keep warm.

7 For sauce, in a saucepan or skillet heat butter or margarine over medium heat till light brown, but not burnt. Pour over ravioli. Sprinkle with cheese and garnish with chives.

The dough and filling can be made up to 24 hours in advance.

NSTA, RICE & PIZZA

Place teaspoonsful of pumpkin filling at 2-inch intervals across the dough.

Brush dough between filling with lightly beaten egg.

Press second sheet of dough between filling to seal.

Use a floured crimped pastry wheel to cut into squares.

Spinach, Cheese, and Pancetta Pasta Shells

Preparation time:
  30 minutes
Cooking time:
  10 minutes
Serves 4

---

16 dried jumbo pasta shells
1 onion, chopped
4 ounces pancetta or Canadian bacon, chopped
2 cloves garlic, crushed
1 tablespoon olive oil
12 large spinach leaves, chopped
2 ripe tomatoes, peeled and chopped
8 ounces ricotta cheese

¼ cup chopped fresh basil
¼ teaspoon ground nutmeg
freshly grated Parmesan

Tomato Sauce
14½-ounce can whole tomatoes
1 tablespoon tomato paste
1 teaspoon sugar

---

1 Cook pasta shells till al dente. Drain; rinse with cold water.
2 In a skillet cook onion, pancetta, and garlic in oil till onion is tender.

3 Add spinach and tomatoes to onion mixture. Cook and stir till tender. Remove from heat.
4 Stir ricotta cheese, basil, and nutmeg

into spinach mixture. Spoon into cooked pasta shells and place in a single layer in a greased shallow baking pan. Bake, uncovered, in a 350° oven for 10 minutes or till heated through. Sprinkle with Parmesan and serve with Tomato Sauce.
5 For Tomato Sauce, place undrained tomatoes in a food processor or blender container. Cover and process or blend till smooth. Strain to remove seeds. In a saucepan combine puréed tomatoes, tomato paste, and sugar. Bring to a boil; reduce heat. Cook, uncovered, for 3 minutes.

Cook onion, pancetta or Canadian bacon, and garlic in oil.

Add spinach and tomatoes to onion mixture in skillet.

Stir ricotta cheese, basil, and nutmeg into spinach mixture.

Use a teaspoon to carefully fill pasta shells.

Porcini Mushroom and Onion Risotto

½ ounce sliced dried porcini mushrooms
4 cups chicken broth
¼ cup butter
2 onions, chopped
1 clove garlic, crushed
1 ½ cups arborio rice
4 ounces fresh mushrooms, chopped
⅓ cup grated parmesan cheese
¼ cup chopped parsley

Preparation time:
10 minutes
Cooking time:
45 minutes
Serves 4

1 Soak porcini mushrooms in hot water to cover for 45 minutes; drain. In a saucepan bring chicken broth to a boil; reduce heat.

2 Meanwhile, in a saucepan melt butter over low heat. Cook onion and garlic in butter till tender and brown.

3 Add rice; stir till well combined. Add 1 cup simmering chicken broth to rice mixture; bring to a boil. Cook and stir till almost all of the broth is absorbed.

4 Add another cup of chicken broth; cook and stir till almost all of the broth is absorbed. Add porcini mushrooms and fresh mushrooms and continue adding stock, 1 cup at a time, as directed above. The total cooking time should be about 20 minutes.

5 Once all the broth has been added and absorbed, reduce heat to low. Stir in parmesan cheese and parsley. Cover; cook for 2 minutes and serve immediately.

HINT
Porcini mushrooms are wild mushrooms which impart a very strong flavor. They are available only in dried form at your supermarket or specialty food store. If porcini mushrooms are unavailable, you can substitute an additional 4 ounces fresh button mushrooms.

Add arborio rice to onion and butter mixture.

Pour one cup chicken broth over rice; cook until broth is absorbed.

Add porcini mushrooms and fresh mushrooms to rice mixture.

Stir in parmesan cheese and parsley and cook for 2 minutes.

Traditional Crispy Pizza

Preparation time:
  30 minutes
Cooking time:
  30 minutes
Serves 4

Crust
1 package active dry yeast
2 teaspoons sugar
1 cup warm water (105° to 115°)
3¼ cups all-purpose flour
pinch salt

Topping
¾ cup tomato sauce
4 ounces sliced Italian salami, cut into strips

¼ cup chopped fresh basil
4 ounces small mushrooms, sliced
1 onion, sliced into thin wedges
½ green bell pepper, sliced
12 pitted ripe olives, halved
6 canned anchovy fillets, drained
1¼ cups shredded mozzarella cheese
⅓ cup grated Parmesan cheese

---

1 For crust, in a bowl combine yeast and sugar. Stir in warm water. Let stand till yeast dissolves.

2 In another bowl stir together flour and salt. Add yeast mixture and stir till well combined. Turn dough out onto a lightly floured surface and knead for 10 minutes or till smooth and elastic.

3 Roll dough to a circle large enough to fit a 12-inch round pizza pan. Transfer dough to pizza pan.

4 Spread dough with tomato sauce and top with salami, basil, mushrooms, onion, bell pepper, olives, and anchovies. Sprinkle with cheeses.

5 Bake, uncovered, in a 375° oven for 30 minutes or till crust is crispy and topping is heated through.

Add yeast, sugar, and water to flour mixture.

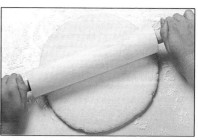

Using a rolling pin, roll dough to a 12-inch circle.

Spread tomato sauce evenly over dough.

Sprinkle topping evenly over pizza. Lay anchovies on top.

MEAT & CHICKEN

*Italy is famous for its veal dishes. In this chapter we include quick and easy recipes
for Veal Scaloppine and Veal with Sage and Lemon.*

Beef and Fresh Mozzarella Salad with Pesto Dressing

Preparation time:
25 minutes
Cooking time:
20 minutes
Serves 4

---

*1 pound eye round
roast or beef
tenderloin*
freshly ground pepper
1 tablespoon olive oil
2 tablespoons butter
*4 ounces fresh
mozzarella cheese
balls*
*8 marinated
artichoke hearts*
*4 bottled roasted red
peppers or pimientos*

*8 radicchio lettuce
leaves*

Pesto Dressing
2/3 cup olive oil
*1/3 cup firmly packed
Italian parsley*
*1/3 cup firmly packed
fresh basil leaves*
*1 tablespoon lemon
juice*
1 tablespoon capers

---

1 Tie beef with string to help hold its shape during cooking; sprinkle with pepper. In a skillet heat oil and butter. Brown meat in hot oil mixture on all sides. Transfer to a shallow baking pan and bake, uncovered, in a 375° oven for 20 minutes. Cool. Remove string and thinly slice.
2 Slice mozzarella cheese, drain and halve artichoke hearts; drain roasted peppers and cut into strips. Arrange on a serving platter with radicchio and beef.
3 For dressing, in a food processor combine oil, parsley, basil, lemon juice, and capers. Process till smooth. Drizzle over salad.

Place meat in a hot skillet and cook on all sides till brown.

Halve artichoke hearts and thinly slice mozzarella balls.

Cut the roasted red peppers or
pimientos into long thin strips.

For dressing, combine oil, parsley,
basil, lemon juice, and capers.

Veal Scaloppine with Eggplant and Tomato

Preparation time:
  25 minutes
Cooking time:
  20 minutes
Serves 4

4 large pieces veal scaloppine (about 1 pound)
all-purpose flour
¼ cup butter
1 small eggplant, thinly sliced
1 large tomato, sliced
4 slices fontina cheese
2 teaspoons dried oregano, crushed
freshly ground pepper

1 Dust veal with flour. In a large skillet melt butter over medium heat until it begins to brown. Add veal in a single layer. Brown quickly in hot butter about 1 minute on each side. Remove.
2 Add eggplant to skillet. Brown on both sides. Remove.
3 Lay one piece of veal on each of four sheets of aluminum foil. Top with eggplant, tomato and cheese. Sprinkle with oregano and pepper.
4 Bring foil loosely up around veal. Seal foil at top, leaving space between foil and cheese. Place foil packages on a baking sheet. Bake in 350° oven 20 minutes. Remove from foil and serve.

Dust veal with flour and quickly brown on both sides in butter.

Lay veal, eggplant, and tomato slices over large sheets of foil.

Place sliced cheese over tomato and sprinkle with oregano.

Bring foil up loosely around veal to form a package.

39

Veal Chops with Sage and Lemon

Preparation time:
   10 minutes
Cooking time:
   10 minutes
Serves 4

4 veal loin chops
all-purpose flour
1 egg, beaten
¼ cup milk
1 cup fine dry bread
   crumbs
1 tablespoon chopped
   fresh sage or
   1 teaspoon dried
2 tablespoons butter
1 tablespoon olive oil
1 clove garlic,
   crushed
lemon wedges

1 Trim fat from chops. Curl up tail of each chop and secure with toothpicks.
2 Dust chops with flour. In a small bowl combine egg and milk. In another bowl combine bread crumbs and sage. Brush egg mixture over chops; coat with bread crumb mixture.
3 In a skillet heat butter, oil and garlic over medium heat. Add chops and cook for 2 to 3 minutes on each side. Serve with lemon wedges.

HINT
To make dried bread crumbs, bake slices of stale bread in a 300° oven until crisp. Using a rolling pin or food processor, crush into crumbs.

Curl up veal chops and secure with toothpicks.

Brush each veal chop with egg mixture.

Coat each veal chop evenly with bread
crumb mixture.

Add chops to skillet in a single layer
and cook over medium heat.

41

Prosciutto Chicken with Anchovy Butter

Preparation time:
30 minutes
Cooking time:
20 minutes
Serves 4

---

1 pound boneless skinless chicken breasts, cut into 4 portions
½ cup chopped parsley
⅓ cup grated parmesan cheese
¼ cup sour cream
2 cloves garlic, crushed
2 teaspoons finely shredded lemon peel

4 slices prosciutto
⅔ cup dry white wine

Anchovy Butter
4 egg yolks
4 canned anchovy fillets, drained
1 tablespoon lemon juice
2 teaspoons prepared mustard
½ cup butter, melted

---

1 Using a meat mallet, flatten chicken breasts slightly. Place breasts, cut side up, on a work surface.
2 In a bowl combine parsley, parmesan, sour cream, garlic, and lemon peel. Spread over the bottom half of each chicken breast. Cut prosciutto slices crosswise in half; lay a piece over the parsley mixture on each breast.
3 Fold chicken breasts in half over filling. Secure with toothpicks. Place in a single layer in a baking dish; pour wine over. Cover; bake in a 350° oven 20 minutes or till no pink remains. Drain.
4 For Anchovy Butter, in a food processor combine egg yolks, anchovies, lemon juice and mustard. Process till smooth. With motor running, pour in butter and blend till well combined. Transfer to saucepan. Cook and stir over low heat till heated through. Pour over chicken and serve immediately.

Spread the bottom half of each chicken breast with parsley mixture.

Place prosciutto over parsley mixture. Fold chicken breasts in half; secure.

Place chicken in a baking dish and pour in wine.

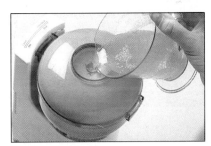

Pour melted butter or margarine into food processor.

43

Braised Chicken in Lemon, Garlic and Rosemary

Preparation time:
  20 minutes
Cooking time:
  40 minutes
Serves 4

3-pound whole chicken
¼ cup olive oil
2 tablespoons butter
1 tablespoon fresh
  rosemary or
  1 teaspoon dried
4 cloves garlic, crushed

2 small red chilies,
  chopped
⅔ cup dry white wine
⅔ cup chicken broth
  strips of peel from
  ½ lemon
⅓ cup lemon juice

---

1 Cut up chicken. Rinse; pat dry.
2 In a large skillet heat oil and butter over medium heat. Add chicken pieces in a single layer; cook till brown.
3 Add rosemary, garlic and chilies to skillet. Stir in wine. Bring to a boil; reduce heat. Cover; simmer 40 minutes.
4 Remove chicken and keep warm. Skim fat from surface of liquid in skillet. Add chicken broth, lemon strips and juice. Bring to a boil. Cook, uncovered, 3 minutes. Pour over chicken.

Brown chicken in oil and butter, turning to prevent sticking.

Pour wine over chicken, rosemary, garlic, and chilies.

Remove cooked chicken from pan using a slotted spoon.

Add broth to skillet with lemon peel and lemon juice. Simmer for 3 minutes.

Olive and Pepper-Stuffed Chicken

8 boneless skinless chicken thighs (about 1 pound)
1/2 of 7-ounce jar roasted whole peppers or 8 pimientos, drained
12 pitted ripe olives
12 pitted green olives
1 small red chili, halved and seeded
6 large basil leaves
1 clove garlic
2 tablespoons butter
1 tablespoon cooking oil
1 1/4 cups water or dry white wine

Preparation time:
    15 minutes
Cooking time:
    15 minutes
Serves 4

1 Lay chicken, cut side up, on a work surface. Use a meat mallet to flatten each thigh slightly.

2 Cut peppers or pimientos into pieces large enough to cover one half of each chicken thigh.

3 In a food processor or blender, combine olives, chili, basil and garlic. Cover and process till finely chopped (or chop olives, chili, basil, and garlic by hand.) Spoon olive mixture over roasted peppers.

4 Fold chicken thighs in half over olive mixture. Secure with toothpicks.

5 In a large skillet heat butter and oil over low heat. Add chicken thighs in a single layer. Increase heat to medium and cook on each side till brown. Use a spatula to loosen chicken from bottom of skillet to prevent sticking.

6 Add water or wine to skillet. Bring to a boil; reduce heat. Cover and simmer for 10 to 15 minutes or till chicken is tender and no pink remains. Serve with pan juices.

HINT
Whole roasted peppers or pimientos are cooked and peeled before being canned or bottled. Use them in salads and casseroles.

Place chicken between two sheets of plastic wrap; flatten with a meat mallet.

Finely chop olives, chili, basil, and garlic by hand or in a food processor.

Spoon olive mixture over pepper or pimiento. Fold chicken and secure.

Pour water or wine over chicken. Cover and simmer till done.

47

SEAFOOD

Almost completely surrounded by sea, Italy enjoys much varied seafood. Fresh fish is enhanced with lemon, olive oil, and aged vinegars.

Peppered Prawns with Fennel

Preparation time:
25 minutes
Cooking time:
10 minutes
Serves 4 to 6

3 pounds prawns or large shrimp
2 tablespoons butter
1 tablespoon olive oil
1 onion, in 8 wedges
1 red bell pepper, cut into strips

1 fennel bulb, sliced
2 cloves garlic, crushed
1 tablespoon freshly ground pepper
¼ cup brandy
1 tablespoon tomato paste

1 Peel and devein prawns, leaving tail intact.
2 In a skillet heat butter and oil. Gently cook onion, bell pepper and fennel till tender.
3 Add prawns, garlic and pepper. Cook till prawns turn pink.
4 Add brandy and paste; cook 1 minute.

Peel and devein prawns or shrimp, leaving tails intact.

Cook onion, fennel and red bell pepper in a skillet till tender.

Add prawns, garlic and pepper. Cook and stir for 3 minutes.

Add brandy and tomato paste to skillet. Cook and stir for 1 minute more.

Fried Smelt with Chili and Herb Mayonnaise

Preparation time:
30 minutes
Cooking time:
10 minutes
Serves 4

---

1 pound whole dressed smelt or catfish strips
all-purpose flour
1 egg, lightly beaten
⅓ cup milk
cooking oil for deep-fat frying

Mayonnaise
⅔ cup mayonnaise or salad dressing

2 red chilies or jalepeno peppers, finely chopped
2 teaspoons lemon juice
2 teaspoons chopped parsley
2 teaspoons chopped fresh basil or ½ teaspoon dried
2 teaspoons chopped capers

---

1 Rinse smelt or catfish and pat dry. Dust fish with flour. In a bowl combine egg and milk. Dip fish in egg mixture.
2 Fry fish in batches in deep hot oil (375°) about 1 minute or till golden brown. Remove and drain on paper towels. Keep warm in a 300° oven while frying the remaining fish.
3 For Chili and Herb Mayonnaise: In a bowl combine mayonnaise or salad dressing, red chilies or jalepeno peppers, lemon juice, parsley, basil and capers. If desired, cover and chill till serving time. Serve as a dip with the fried smelt or catfish.
Variation: Squid or calamari can replace the smelt. Slice squid into thin strips and dust with flour. Dip into egg mixture and coat with fine dry bread crumbs. Fry as directed above.

> ## HINT
> To keep herbs fresh, wrap them in a damp towel and store them in the refrigerator.

Dip floured smelt or catfish into egg mixture.

Add fish in small batches to hot oil and cook until golden brown.

Use a large metal strainer to remove fish from hot oil.

Add chilies, lemon juice, parsley, basil, and capers to mayonnaise.

Fresh Tuna with Herbs and Balsamic Vinegar

4 tuna steaks, cut about 1/2 inch thick
1/4 cup olive oil
1 tablespoon chopped parsley
1 tablespoon chopped fresh basil or 1 teaspoon dried
1/4 cup balsamic vinegar

Preparation time:
  5 minutes
Cooking time:
  10 minutes
Serves 4

1 Rinse tuna and pat dry with paper towels. In a large skillet heat oil over medium heat. Add tuna to hot oil and cook for 4 to 6 minutes or till fish flakes easily when tested with a fork, turning steaks once.
2 Transfer tuna to a serving plate.

Sprinkle with parsley and basil; drizzle with balsamic vinegar.

HINT
Balsamic vinegar comes from Modena in Italy. It is made from unfermented white wine grapes and aged in the same way as wine, giving it a rich flavor. Balsamic vinegar is 20 years old before it is sold. Look for balsamic vinegar at the supermarket with other cooking vinegars or at specialty food stores. Red wine vinegar may be substituted.

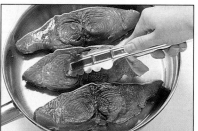

Put tuna in a large skillet in a single layer.

Turn tuna steaks once to cook both sides.

Place tuna steaks on a platter and sprinkle with basil.

Spoon balsamic vinegar over tuna and serve immediately.

DESSERTS & CAKE

*Desserts are sweet and lush or simply elegant
in the Italian cuisine. Traditional favorites are found
in this mouthwatering chapter.*

Lemon Zabaglione

*3 egg yolks
1/4 cup sugar
1/2 cup dry white wine
1/4 cup lemon juice
1 tablespoon Marsala
8 almond cookies
fresh strawberries
(optional)*

Preparation time:
5 minutes
Cooking time:
10 minutes
Serves 4

1 In a heatproof
bowl beat egg yolks
and sugar with a wire
whisk until light and
creamy. Add white
wine, lemon juice and
Marsala. Whisk until
well combined.
2 Place bowl over
a saucepan of
simmering water,
making sure that
bottom of bowl does
not touch water.
Cook and stir for
10 minutes or till
mixture thickens.
3 Spoon into
decorative serving
glasses and serve
with cookies and
strawberries.

*Whisk egg yolks and sugar in a
heatproof bowl until creamy.*

*Pour in wine, lemon juice, and
Marsala. Whisk well.*

Place bowl over simmering water, stirring until thickened.

Spoon zabaglione into serving glasses and serve with biscuits.

Tirami Su

4 egg yolks
1/3 cup sugar
1/3 cup milk
8 ounces mascarpone
3 egg whites
8 ounces lady fingers
1 3/4 cups cold coffee
1 tablespoon
    unsweetened cocoa
    powder
fresh strawberries
    (optional)

Preparation time:
    20 minutes
Cooking time:
    5 minutes
Chilling time:
    6 hours or
    overnight
Serves 6

1 In a heatproof bowl beat egg yolks and sugar with an electric mixer till light and creamy. Add milk and beat till well combined.

2 Place bowl over a saucepan of simmering water, making sure that bottom of bowl does not touch water. Cook and stir for 5 minutes or till mixture thickens. Remove from heat and cool.

3 Stir mascarpone into egg yolk mixture until well combined. In another bowl beat egg whites with an electric mixer till soft peaks form; fold into mascarpone mixture.

4 Dip lady fingers quickly into coffee so they are moist but not soggy. Place one-fourth of the lady fingers on the bottom of a waxed paper-lined 9 x 5 x 3-inch loaf pan. Spread with one-third of the mascarpone mixture. Repeat layering with lady fingers and mascarpone, ending with lady fingers.

5 Cover and chill for at least 6 hours or preferably overnight. To serve, invert mixture onto a serving plate; remove waxed paper. Sift cocoa powder over the top and slice to serve. If desired, serve with strawberries.

Add mascarpone to egg mixture; stir till well combined.

Fold egg whites into egg mixture using a metal spoon.

Dip lady fingers quickly into hot coffee.
They should be moist but not soggy.

Repeat layers of mascarpone mixture
and lady fingers.

Lemon-Lime Italian Ice

2½ cups water
1¼ cups sugar
1 cup lemon juice
1 cup lime juice
8-ounce carton lemon
  yogurt

Preparation time:
  25 minutes
Cooking time:
  10 minutes
Freezing time:
  1–2 hours plus
  overnight
Serves 6

1 In a saucepan combine water and sugar. Cook and stir over low heat till sugar dissolves. Bring to a boil; reduce heat. Simmer, uncovered, for 10 minutes; cool.
2 Add lemon and lime juice to syrup in saucepan. Pour mixture into a large shallow container. Freeze for 1 to 2 hours or till firm but not solid.
3 Transfer mixture to a food processor or blender container. Add yogurt and cover and process or blend till smooth. Return to freezer container overnight or till firm.

HINT
Any fresh citrus juices besides lemon and lime can be used either alone or in combination. Try orange, grapefruit, tangerine, or tangelo.

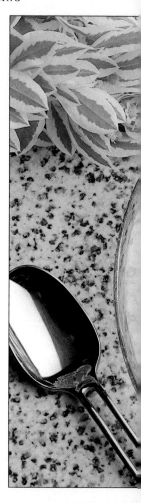

Stir sugar and water over low heat till sugar dissolves.

Add lemon juice and lime juice to cooled syrup.

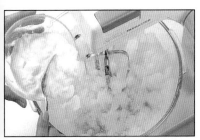

Beat frozen mixture with an electric mixer. Beat in yogurt.

Return mixture to freezer container and freeze till firm.

Chocolate Ricotta Torte

Preparation time:
  30 minutes
Cooking time:
  40 minutes
Serves 8

Cake
1/2 cup butter, softened
1 cup plus
  2 tablespoons sugar
2 eggs
1 1/3 cups self-rising
  flour
2/3 cup unsweetened
  cocoa powder
1 cup water

Filling
8 ounces ricotta cheese
1 ounce candied
  mixed peel, finely
  chopped (1/4 cup)

1 ounce candied
  cherries, finely
  chopped (1/4 cup)
1/4 cup sugar

Topping
2 teaspoons instant
  coffee powder
1 teaspoon hot water
1 1/4 cups heavy
  cream
2 tablespoons
  powdered sugar
6 tablespoons brandy
1 cup slivered
  almonds, toasted

1 For the cake, in a bowl beat butter with an electric mixer till smooth. Add sugar and beat till fluffy. Beat in eggs, one at a time, till well combined. Stir together flour and cocoa powder. Add flour mixture and water alternately to batter, beating till smooth. Beat for 2 to 3 minutes more or till light and fluffy.

2 Pour batter into a greased and lightly floured 8-inch cake pan. Bake in a 350° oven for 40 minutes or till a toothpick inserted near the center comes out clean. Cool on a wire rack for 10 minutes. Remove from pan and cool thoroughly on wire rack. Cut cake into three layers.

3 For filling, in a bowl stir together ricotta cheese, mixed peel, sugar and cherries.

4 For topping, dissolve coffee in water. In a bowl beat cream, coffee mixture and powdered sugar with an electric mixer till soft peaks form.

5 To assemble torte, place one cake layer on a serving plate. Brush with 2 tablespoons of the brandy and spread with half the ricotta filling. Top with another cake layer; brush with 2 tablespoons brandy and spread with remaining ricotta filling. Top with last cake layer and brush with remaining brandy. Spread top and sides with whipped cream mixture. Sprinkle almonds around top edge of the cake.

Slice the cake horizontally into three layers.

Combine ricotta cheese, sugar, mixed peel and cherries.

Spread ricotta mixture evenly between cake layers.

Spread the top and sides of the cake with the coffee whipped cream.

GLOSSARY

Anchovies Small saltwater fish. Can occasionally be bought fresh but usually available in cans. Their flavor is strong. For a milder flavor, soak in milk about 20 minutes before using.

Arborio rice Large-grained Italian white rice, ideal for making risotto. Look for arborio rice at Italian markets or specialty food stores.

Arugula Also known as rocket lettuce, arugula is used in salads or sautéed. It has a peppery flavor.

Balsamic vinegar Originally from Modena, Italy, it is aged like wine, giving it a well-rounded and rich flavor.

Capers Flower buds of the caper bush, capers are usually pickled in vinegar.

Cheeses

Bocconcini Fresh mozzarella cheese, molded into small patties or rounds.

Ideal for antipasto and salads.

Feta Crumbly cheese with a robust flavor. Made from sheep's, goat's or cow's milk and stored in brine.

Fontina Soft buttery cheese from Val d'Aosta, Northern Italy. Ideal for melting.

Gorgonzola Creamy blue-veined cheese with a pungent flavor, originally from Lombardy.

Mozzarella Smooth, soft, elastic cheese with a mild flavor. Ideal for melting.

Parmesan Hard cheese bought in blocks or wedges. For best flavor, store in refrigerator but serve at room temperature. Grate only as you need it.

Pecorino Similar to Parmesan cheese, made from sheep's or cow's milk with a rich, tangy flavor.

Ricotta Fresh, unripened cheese made during the manufacture of other cheeses. It has a soft creamy texture and a mild, sweet flavor.

Herbs Fresh herbs will give the best and most authentic flavor to Italian cooking. To keep herbs fresh, wrap them in a clean, damp towel and store in the refrigerator.

Lady fingers Also called savoiardi biscuits, they are wide, flat, sponge finger cookies.

Marsala Sweet, fortified wine, originally made near Marsala, Italy.

Mascarpone Sometimes referred to as a cheese, mascarpone is made by adding an acid ingredient, such as lemon juice, to cream. The mixture is allowed to stand until it clots and the excess liquid is strained off. It has a soft creamy texture and a slightly acidic flavor, similar to sour cream.

Olives Fruit of the olive tree, either picked green or fully ripened and black.

Olive oil The preferred oil for Italian cooking. It comes in the following three grades:

1. Extra virgin olive oil – the best quality, made from the first cold pressing of the olives. Greenish in color, this thick oil is used in salads and other dishes where flavor is important.

2. Virgin olive oil – made from the second cold pressing of the olives. Gold in color and moderately thick, this oil is used for marinades, mayonnaise, and general cooking.

3. Olive oil – made from the third pressing of the olives with heat being applied to extract the oil. A light oil, pale gold in color and best used for general cooking and deep-fat frying.

Pancetta Pork belly that is salted, cured, and spiced. It can be eaten as it is or cooked with other ingredients.

Pasta A flour and water dough sometimes with the addition of eggs. The dough is molded into a huge variety of shapes. Pasta can be homemade or purchased fresh from pasta shops or supermarkets. Quality varies, but as a guide, look for pasta made from durum wheat for the best texture and ease of handling.

Polenta Also called coarse cornmeal, polenta is used to make a porridge-like mixture that is served with meals or made into a type of bread that is baked or fried.

Porcini mushrooms Wild mushrooms, imported in a dry form. They have a strong flavor and are used sparingly.

Prosciutto Uncooked, unsmoked leg of pork that is cured in salt. Can be eaten as is or cooked with other ingredients.

Roasted peppers or pimientos Pimiento is Spanish for bell pepper. The peppers are peeled, then preserved in water or oil.

Sambuca A colorless liqueur with aniseed flavor, traditionally served in liqueur glasses with three coffee beans. It is set aflame to roast the beans and release the flavor.

Squid tubes Also known as calamari tubes, these are small squid which have been cleaned and skinned.

Tomatoes For best flavor, use only ripe tomatoes. Tomatoes should be ripened at room temperature, not in the refrigerator.

INDEX